PREDATOR VS PREY

HOW LIONS AND OTHER MAMMALS ATTACK

TIM HARRIS

PowerKiDS press

Published in 2026
by The Rosen Publishing Group, Inc.
2544 Clinton Street, Buffalo, NY 14224

First published in Great Britain in 2021 by Wayland

Editor: Amy Pimperton
Design: www.smartdesignstudio.co.uk
Picture research: Diana Morris

Cataloging-in-Publication Data

Names: Harris, Tim.

Title: How lions and other mammals attack / Tim Harris.

Description: Buffalo, NY : PowerKids Press, 2026. | Series: Predator vs. prey | Includes glossary and index.

Identifiers: ISBN 9781499454246 (pbk.) | ISBN 9781499454253 (library bound) | ISBN 9781499454260 (ebook)

Subjects: LCSH: Predatory animals--Behavior--Juvenile literature.

Classification: LCC QL758.H377 2026 | DDC
591.53--dc23

Picture credits:
Dreamstime:Steffen Foerster 9b. FLPA Images: Dembinsky Photo Ass 22. iStock: Datmore 18.Nature PL: John Abbott 29t; Franco Banfi 19t; Espen Bergersen 1bc, 4b, 19b; Michael Durham 28; Sue Eszterhas 25b; Andy Rouse 1bl, 21b; Staffan Widstrand 11t.Shutterstock: Africa Wildlife 1br, 13b; Steve Byland 23b; Vlada Cech front cover tl; Norma Cornes 5c, 24; Jim Cumming 5br; Robert Eastman 23t; Iakov Filimonov 14; Gaidamashchuk 7cl; Giedriius 2br, 7t; Leonardo Gonzalez 27t; GoodStudio 29cr; GTW back cover tl, 5t, 11b; Eric Isselee 12, 17t, 31b; Ammit Jack 6; Rosa Jay 25t; Anan Kaewkhammul 3tc, 21t; Tory Kallman 26; Macrovector 23cr; Marques 10; Maquilladora 29cl; Leonardo Mercon 2bc, 17b; Nadya_Art 7cr, 9c, 11c, 13c, 15c, 17cl, 19c, 21cl, 23cl, 25cr, 27cl; Nejron Photo front cover c; Cheryl Nelson 2bl, 15t; Notion Pic 17cr, 25cl; Nwdph 3tl, 7b;Franck Palaticky 3tr, 15b; Prapass 13t; Ondrej Prosicky 16; Mariat S 20; Olga Serova 27cr; Southtownboy Studio 9t; Veronika Surovyseva 8, 30t; The Len back cover tc, 4c; John Tunney 27b; Sergey Uryadnikov front cover tr; Rudmer Zwerver back cover tr, 5bl, 29b.

Manufactured in the United States of America

CPSIA Compliance Information: Batch #CSPK26. For further information contact Rosen Publishing at 1-800-237-9932.

CONTENTS

MAMMAL PREDATORS

Mammals are a type of animal. They have fur or hair (believe it or not, dolphins are born with whiskers on their jaws). Almost all give birth to live babies rather than lay eggs and, as young, they feed on their mother's milk. Many mammals are herbivores and eat plants. Plenty of other mammals are carnivores and eat meat. They must hunt and kill prey animals to survive.

Mammal predators live in all kinds of different places – on land and in the oceans. They vary in size, from tiny shrews to large, fearsome tigers and giant whales. They are adapted to their habitats and to thrive on the prey they hunt.

Many predators share some common features, such as forward-facing eyes with binocular vision. Senses are important. Predators often have excellent senses of hearing, smell, or eyesight.

BENGAL TIGER

ORCA

POLAR BEAR

CHIMPANZEE

Some mammals that have no natural enemies apart from humans are called apex predators. But some predators are hunted by bigger predators. Sometimes these bigger predators are eaten by even larger ones! This is called a food chain.

GREY WOLF

PIPISTRELLE BAT

This book looks at the extraordinary ways some mammals go about hunting and killing their prey. Some use brute force, others use tools, some have special adaptations, such as echolocation, and others may use speed or ambush. Read on to find out more.

JAGUAR VS. CAIMAN: JAWS

Jaguars are big cats with a beautiful pattern of black rings and dots on their fur. They are some of the most fearsome predators on Earth. Tigers and lions are both larger cat species, but a jaguar's bite is more powerful. A jaguar's big, sharp teeth can break through the thick shell of a turtle with ease. These cats aren't fussy eaters: they also kill deer, cattle, horses, monkeys, fish, and birds. Pretty much anything, in fact – as long as it's meat!

STALK AND AMBUSH

Jaguars live in forests and swamps in South America. Mostly, they hunt alone. They are secretive stalk-and-ambush predators, which means they creep up silently on their victims – then pounce! They are excellent swimmers and their diet includes aquatic animals, such as anaconda snakes and caimans. Jaguars' teeth are strong enough to bite through the tough hide of a caiman.

JAWS: BONES THAT FRAME THE MOUTH AND HOLD THE TEETH

CAIMAN

Caimans are also predators. These reptiles also have strong jaws with long lines of sharp teeth. Most of the time they lie motionless on a riverbank or float unseen in the water. But when prey comes close, a caiman will spring into action, charging forward to grab a capybara or snake. Once caught in its jaws, the victim will not escape. The caiman swallows it in one gulp.

JAGUAR STATS

Length: 3.5-6 ft (1-1.8 m)
Weight: 123-212 lb (56-96 kg)
Top speed: 40 mph (64 kph)

Moves silently; extremely powerful jaws and sharp teeth; excellent senses

VS.

(YACARE) CAIMAN STATS

Length: 4.5-8 ft (1.4-2.4 m)
Weight: 50-128 lb (23-58 kg)
Top speed: 25 mph (40 kph) for very short distances

Excellent swimmer; thick, scaly hide; good hearing and eyesight; strong jaws and teeth

AQUATIC: AN ANIMAL (OR PLANT) THAT LIVES IN OR NEAR WATER

SURPRISE!

A caiman's jaws and teeth could easily injure a jaguar, so the cat has to use surprise, approaching from behind, to limit the danger. Jaguars often kill their prey by biting into the skull, piercing it with four sharp canine teeth.

CHEETAH VS. GAZELLE: SPEED

Cheetahs are the fastest animals on land. These large cats use their speed to hunt on the plains of Africa. When a hungry cheetah sees a herd of gazelles, it will sneak through long savannah grass to get as close as it can. It will choose one gazelle and, when the moment is right, it will explode from cover and sprint toward its prey.

SAVANNAH: TROPICAL GRASSLAND

BUILT FOR SPEED

When the gazelle notices the cat, it will flee as fast as it can. But a cheetah is built for speed and can accelerate from 0 to 60 miles per hour (96.5 kph) in less than three seconds – that's quicker than the fastest car! Its top speed is an incredible 70 miles per hour (113 kph). If it catches up with its prey, the cheetah knocks it off its feet and kills it with a bite to the neck. Cheetahs eat Thomson's gazelles, impala, guinea fowl, and hares.

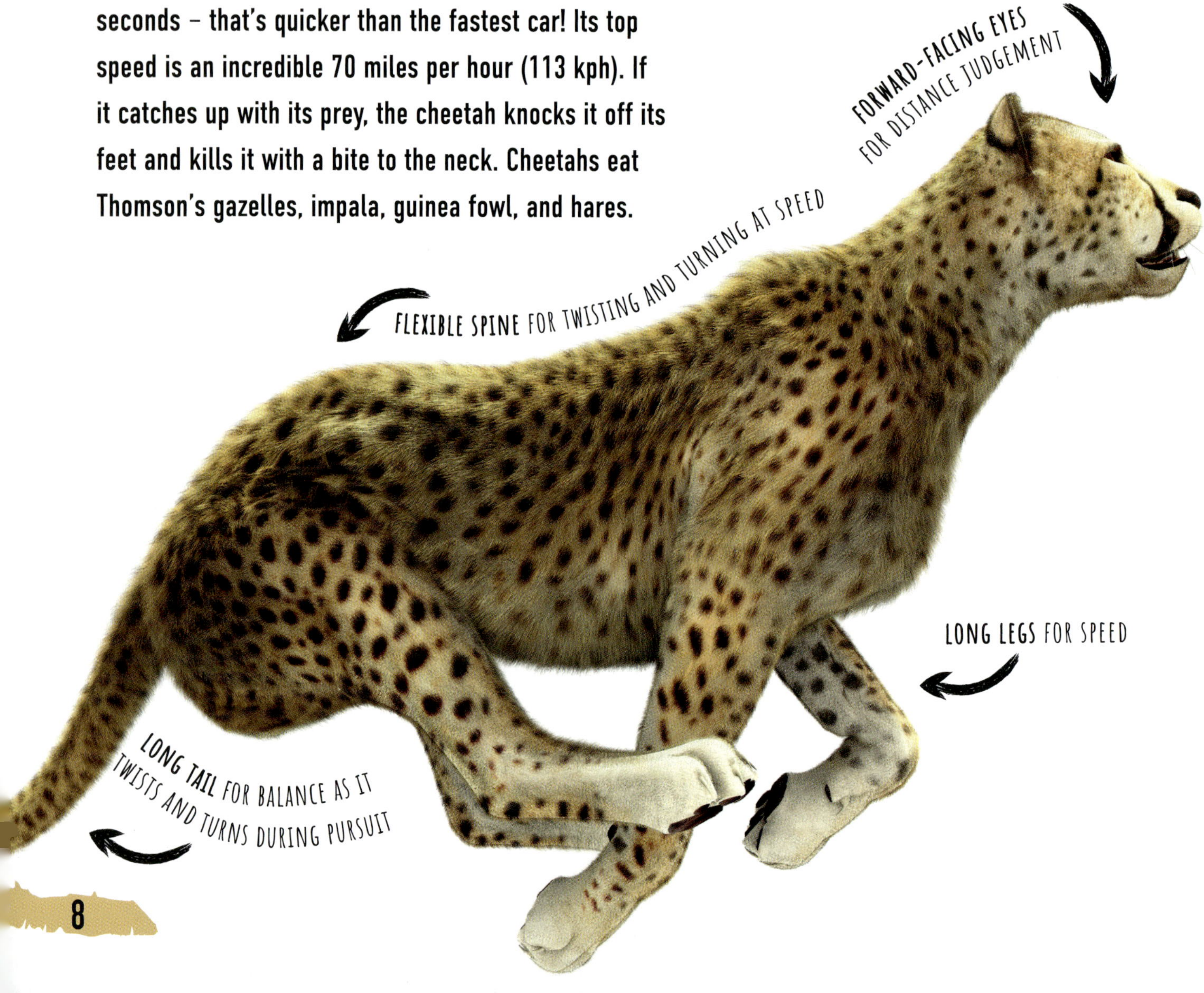

THOMSON'S GAZELLE

Gazelles are very alert. With eyes on the sides of their head, they can see small movements behind them as well as to the side and in front. They also have good senses of hearing and smell. Although not as fast as a cheetah, Thomson's gazelles can still reach 56 miles per hour (90 kph) – and can keep running for longer. Their biggest trick, though, is their ability to zigzag at speed, throwing their pursuer off balance.

CHEETAH STATS	THOMSON'S GAZELLE STATS
Length: 3.5-5 ft (1.1-1.5 m) Weight: 75-141 lb (34-64 kg) Top speed: 70 mph (113 kph)	Length: 2.5-4 ft (0.8-1.2 m) Weight: 55-77 lb (25-35 kg) Top speed: 56 mph (90 kph)

VS.

Extremely fast over short distances but lacks stamina; excellent senses	Fast over long distances, expert zigzagger; excellent senses of sight and smell

MUSCLE STRAIN

A cheetah 's long, springy legs give it a 23-foot (7 m) stride at top speed. As for top athletes, sprinting puts a strain on these cats' muscles, and they sometimes suffer injuries.

DUSK AND DAWN

Sprinting is a hot business on the plains of east Africa, so cheetahs do most of their hunting around dawn and dusk when it is a bit cooler. A cheetah will eat its meal as quickly as possible – before it gets stolen by a hyena or lion.

POLAR BEAR VS. SEAL: SMELL

Polar bears are the top predators of the frozen Arctic. They have strong jaws and terrifying claws, but their most valuable hunting weapon is their nose! They can smell a seal's scent more than half a mile (0.8 km) away. They can even figure out if there's a seal in the water beneath thick ice and snow.

SNIFFING OUT SUPPER

Seals spend much of their life diving for fish in the icy waters of the Arctic Ocean. In winter, the surface of the ocean is frozen, so they have to swim under a sheet of ice. Every so often, though, they need to come to the surface to breathe. Polar bears sniff out where the nearest breathing hole is. There, they wait patiently for a seal to come up for air – then grab it!

SCENT: THE DISTINCTIVE SMELL OF AN ANIMAL

RINGED SEAL

Polar bears need a regular supply of fatty seal blubber to stay alive, but seals are clever. Seals burrow several holes through the ice, so a bear doesn't know which one it will emerge from next. Seals sometimes blow bubbles into the hole before they surface to see if a bear reacts, and they can slip down into the water again very quickly if a bear attacks.

POLAR BEAR STATS

Length: 7-8 ft (2.1-2.4 m)
Weight: 650-1,190 lb (295-540 kg)
Top speed: 25 mph (40 kph) in short bursts

Excellent sense of smell; good eyesight and hearing; extremely powerful

VS.

SEAL STATS

Length: 5 ft (1.5 m)
Weight: 110-154 lb (50-70 kg)
Top speed: Unknown; very slow on land, but fast swimmer

Intelligent; can stay underwater for long periods; good swimmer

BLUBBER: FAT UNDER THE SKIN OF SEA MAMMALS

HUNTING FOR PUPS

In winter, pregnant female ringed seals haul themselves out of the water and dig a lair in the snow where they give birth to a single pup. For six weeks, the pup stays there, feeding on its mother's milk. If a polar bear finds them, it is guaranteed a meal because seal pups are too helpless to escape.

LION VS. ZEBRA: STEALTH

Lions are big cats and awesome predators. They live on the open savanna of Africa in groups called prides. There, they use quiet cunning to catch their prey. It is the females (lionesses) that do most of the hunting. Males that live alone can't rely on lionesses and have to do their own hunting.

CUNNING: GOOD AT FOOLING OTHER ANIMALS

HUNTING LIONESS

Although a lioness is smaller than a male lion, she is better at hunting. That's because she's quicker. Although she is not as fast as a cheetah, she has great acceleration and can twist and turn as she runs. Her front legs are so powerful they can bring down a zebra, wildebeest, or baby elephant. A lioness has jaws that are strong enough to either break her prey's neck or suffocate it.

STEALTH: MOVING SLOWLY AND QUIETLY SO AS NOT TO BE SEEN

ZEBRA

Zebras live in herds, so there are many pairs of eyes and ears to watch and listen for danger. If one zebra senses a predator, it may bark a warning – or simply run. Then all the other zebras will run, too. If the herd stays together, it will be safe. But often one animal – a slower, older one – will get separated and fall victim to the hunter.

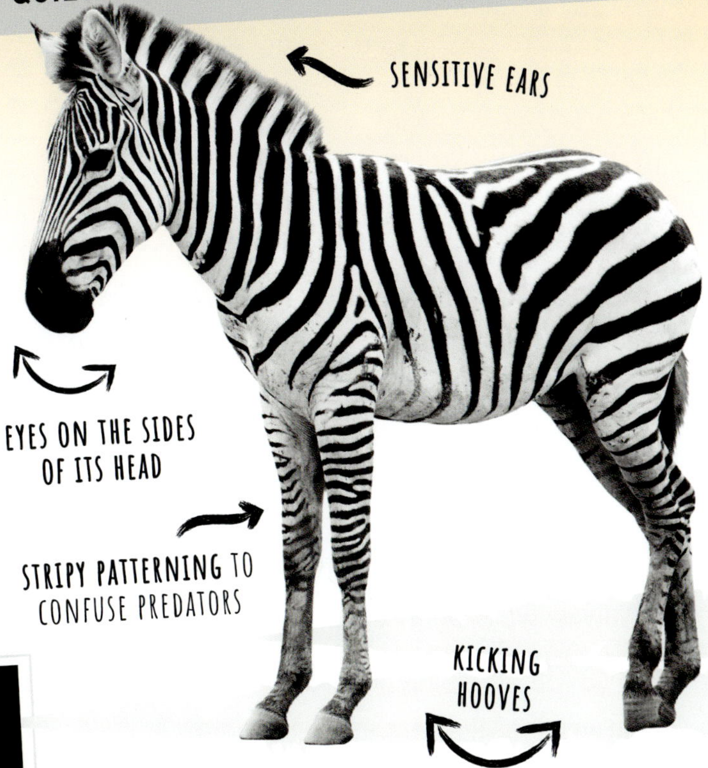

LION STATS

Length: 5-7 ft (1.5-2.1 m)
Weight: 290-420 lb (132-190 kg)
Top speed: 50 mph (80 kph)

Excellent night vision; well-organised teamwork; quick over short distances; very powerful

VS.

ZEBRA STATS

Length: 7-8 ft (2-2.4 m)
Weight: 385-850 lb (175-385 kg)
Top speed: 40 mph (64 kph)

Excellent senses of vision, hearing,and smell; stamina when running

STEALTH AND TEAMWORK

Lions usually hunt in a group at night. They silently stalk their prey and then fan out, cutting off escape routes. The males often herd their intended prey to move toward the deadly females! Then the moment comes to attack.

IN FOR THE KILL

As the lionesses spring forward, the startled animals will panic. If one becomes separated from the rest of the herd it makes an easier target for the big cats. After a brief chase, a lioness will knock the unlucky creature off balance and clamp strong jaws around its throat, cutting off the air supply and suffocating it.

WOLF VS. MOOSE: STAMINA

Wolves are social animals, living in groups called packs. Because they also hunt in groups, working together they can tackle animals much bigger than themselves, including bison and very large deer called moose. Although they usually target moose that are old or ill, they sometimes use teamwork and stamina to kill a healthy animal.

HARDY: ABLE TO LIVE IN HARSH CONDITIONS

HARDY ANIMALS

Wolves live in many parts of the world, including the far north of Canada and Russia. There, it is bitterly cold for much of the year and finding prey is not easy. When a pack does find a suitable target, it will approach as closely as possible. When their prey realizes the threat, it may run and the wolves give chase.

The pursuit may be over in a few minutes, but it may last for hours because wolves do not tire easily. Their strong, long legs allow them to keep moving at a speed of 6 miles per hour (10 kph) for several hours, even in deep snow.

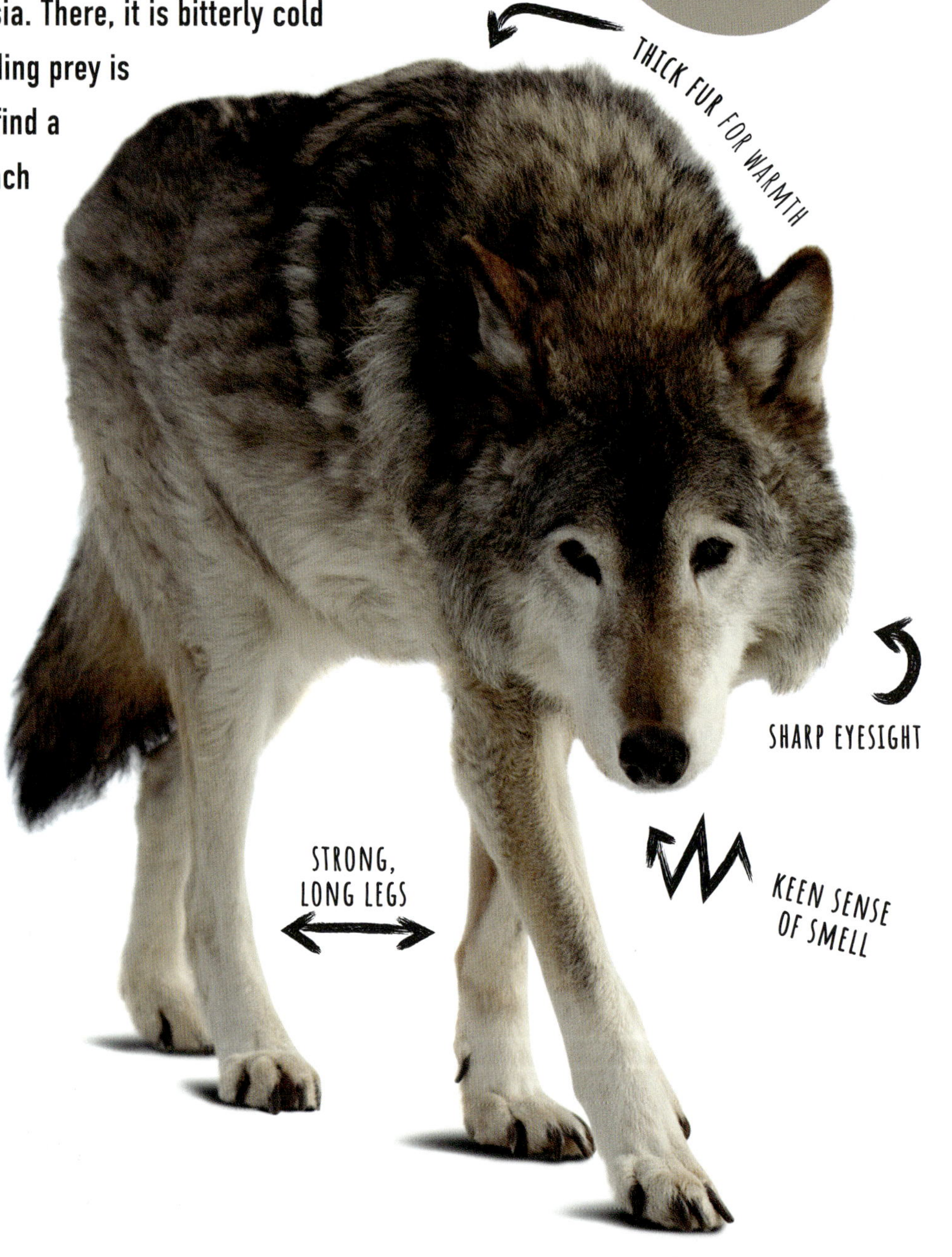

STAMINA: BEING ABLE TO DO SOMETHING FOR A LONG TIME

MOOSE

A fit adult elk is a formidable opponent for any predator. Standing 7 feet (2 m) tall, elk have long legs that they can kick in all directions. A blow from one of their hard hooves will send an attacker reeling. An elk may even charge a predator with its large antlers.

WOLF STATS

Length: 4-5.5 ft (1.2-1.7 m)
Weight: 77-99 lb (35-45 kg)
Top speed: 40 mph (65 kph)

Stamina; well-organised teamwork; great senses of smell, eyesight and hearing

VS.

MOOSE STATS

Length: 1.7-2.3 m
Weight: 827-1,600 lb (375-725 kg)
Top speed: 22 mph (35 kph)

Very large; male has large antlers; long legs with hard hooves kick backward, forward, and sideways

SHARING THE FEAST

When a pack of wolves has killed a large animal, every member of the group shares the feast. Adult wolves eat in order, with the alpha male and female tucking in first. Adults regurgitate fresh meat to feed the pups. Each wolf can eat as much as 4 pounds (11 kg) of meat in one sitting. This is important because it may be a long time before they get to eat again – they can go for up to two weeks without eating.

MARGAY VS. TAMARIN: MIMICRY

Margays are small wild cats that live in the dense forests of South America. They are skillful climbers, moving quickly from branch to branch. They can even hang from a branch by one hind leg! Margays go hunting at night. They search for birds, rats, lizards, tree frogs, and small monkeys called tamarins.

ANIMAL MIMICS

Some animals are mimics – they pretend to be other animals. Some birds copy the songs of other birds to show off; other harmless insects scare off predators by having the same colors as wasps. A hungry margay has an especially sneaky trick: it uses mimicry to lure a victim. Hiding in thick tangles of leaves, it copies the high-pitched squeals of a baby tamarin. Adult monkeys come running to investigate. If one of them gets close enough, the margay will leap out and grab it.

MIMIC: TO COPY OR IMITATE SOMETHING OR SOMEONE

PIED TAMARIN

Tamarins are squirrel-sized monkeys that live in groups called troops. Like margays, they are excellent climbers and have long tails to help them keep their balance high above the ground. While a group of tamarins is feeding, an adult called a sentinel keeps watch. If a predator appears, the sentinel will shout out a warning to his troop, which will flee through the branches at great speed.

SNEAKY: TO DO SOMETHING WITHOUT BEING NOTICED; SLY

MARGAY STATS	(PIED) TAMARIN STATS
Length: 20-31 in (50-79) cm (plus long tail)	**Length:** 8-11 in (20-28 cm) (plus long tail)
Weight: 7 lb (3.2 kg)	**Weight:** 14 oz (400 g)
Top speed: unknown	**Top speed:** 25 mph (40 kph)
Super tree-climber; night vision; great sense of hearing; mimicry	Rapid escape through foliage; use lookouts to watch for danger; sensitive sight, hearing, and sense of smell

OTHER CATS

Other kinds of wild cat hunt monkeys, too, including jaguars and ocelots (right), which look a lot like margays. People who live in remote parts of the Amazon rainforest have heard them mimicking the sounds of birds and other mammals, as well as baby monkeys. So, it may be that they catch a lot of their food in this way, too.

ORCA VS. SPERM WHALE: TEAMWORK

Orcas, or killer whales, are fearsome ocean hunters. Think of what makes the perfect ocean predator: intelligence, powerful jaws, strong teeth, good eyesight, great speed, and swimming skills. An orca has all of these. What makes these marine mammals even more deadly is that they hunt in groups, called pods. Together they track down and kill fish, sea turtles, squid, seals, and even other whales.

GROUP HUNTING

Usually, orcas target smaller prey, but if a pod finds a group of female sperm whales with their baby whales (calves), they may attack. They try to separate the calves from their mothers by chasing them. If a calf does lose the protection of its mother, the orcas move in for the kill, grabbing their victim with their 4-inch (10 cm) long teeth. But orcas do not always get their own way in these battles.

TEAMWORK: WORKING AS A GROUP TO ACHIEVE A GOAL

SPERM WHALE

Sperm whales are large predators themselves – they are bigger than orcas, but are not as aggressive. If attacked, the group protects their calves by forming a defensive ring around them, pointing their powerful tail flukes outward. A blow from a sperm whale's tail can stun even the largest attacker. If a giant male sperm whale is present, the orcas will not attack.

ORCA STATS

Length: 26 ft (8 m)
Weight: 6.6 tons (6 mt)
Top speed: 28 mph (45 kph)

Hunts in a group; strong; intelligent; fast and agile swimmer; good eyesight above and below water

VS.

SPERM WHALE STATS

Length: 36-52 ft (11-16 m)
Weight: 15.4- 44 tons (14-40 mt)
Top speed: 25 mph (40 kph)

Large size; powerful tail; defends in a group; excellent diver; very sensitive hearing

FLUKES: THE TWO FLAT PARTS OF A WHALE'S TAIL

SPYHOPPING

Orcas have a special trick, called spyhopping, that allows them to see what's going on without being spotted by other animals. They submerge their whole body with just their head peeping up above the water so they can look all around them.

TIGER VS. GAUR: AMBUSH

Tigers are the biggest of the big cats and are apex predators in their habitats. These stripy killers are solitary hunters in forests and grasslands in some parts of Asia. There, they hunt large animals, such as deer, buffalo, wild boar, monkeys, and wild cattle called gaur. Sometimes, they even kill young elephants, though attacks on adults are rare.

AMBUSH KILLER

An animal grazing in the forest often doesn't realize that a tiger is creeping up on it, slowly and silently on large padded paws. If the tiger can get within about 25 feet (8 m) of its prey, it stands a good chance of making a kill. Then it will leap from cover and lock its strong jaws around the victim's neck. Unable to breathe, the prey suffocates. Despite its camouflage, stealth, and strength, a tiger ambush is not always successful.

APEX PREDATOR: AN ANIMAL AT THE TOP OF A FOOD CHAIN

AMBUSH: TO HIDE AND LIE IN WAIT BEFORE ATTACKING

GAUR

Gaur are the world's largest wild cattle. Bulls have fearsome, curved horns. A charging gaur could trample most other animals underfoot. If a tiger confronts a group of gaur with their calves, the adults will form a protective ring around them – and the tiger will probably abandon its attack.

TIGER STATS

Length: 8-9.5 ft (2.5-2.9 m)
Weight: 310-485 lb (140-220 kg)
Top speed: 40 mph (64 kph)

Excellent senses; superb camouflage; great strength

VS.

GAUR STATS

Length: 8-11 ft (2.5-3.3 m)
Weight: 2,205 lb (1,000 kg)
Top speed: 30 mph (48 kph)

Very large size; horns

STRIPY CAT

A tiger stands out pretty obviously in a zoo, but in dense undergrowth its stripes give it superb camouflage to hide from prey. Tigers are the only big cats that are completely striped, and the pattern of every individual is slightly different.

AMERICAN SHORT-TAILED SHREW VS. GARTER SNAKE: VENOM

Short-tailed shrews are tiny mammals that live in the leaf-litter of North American forests. They weigh only as much as an AA battery and look very cute, but they are really aggressive killers. These shrews hunt night and day for beetles, earthworms, snails, mice, frogs, salamanders, and even small snakes. They eat up to three times their weight in food every day!

TOXIC SALIVA

It seems extraordinary that these shrews can eat animals that are larger than themselves. They aren't strong enough to overpower large prey – instead, they use deadly poison to do it. A short-tailed shrew's saliva contains enough toxic chemicals to kill 200 mice. When it bites its prey, the saliva enters the wound, gets into the animal's bloodstream and paralyzes it. Unable to move, the shrew's victim cannot escape. It is eaten on the spot or dragged off to be munched at leisure later.

PARALYZED: WHEN A BODY (OR PART OF IT) CAN'T MOVE

VENOM: POISON INJECTED INTO PREY

FLICKING TONGUE FOR SENSING PREDATORS OR PREY

GARTER SNAKE

Garter snakes are also predators, and they eat the same kinds of animals as shrews. They have teeth to grab prey and can swallow mice, reptiles, and frogs in one gulp. However, unlike shrews, their weaponry does not include strong venom. If a shrew bites a snake before the snake can bite the shrew – the shrew is likely to be the winner.

SHORT-TAILED SHREW STATS

Length: 4 in (10 cm)
Weight: 1 oz (30 g)
Top speed: unknown

Echolocation; venomous saliva

VS.

GARTER SNAKE STATS

Length: 18-22 in (45-55 cm)
Weight: 5 oz (140 g)
Top speed: unknown

Fast when escaping predators; mild venom

A SHORT-TAILED SHREW'S EARS ARE HIDDEN IN ITS DENSE, VELVETY FUR.

EARS NOT EYES

Short-tailed shrews have tiny eyes and terrible eyesight. They find their way around mostly by listening to the echoes of their high-pitched squeaks to figure out if there's an obstacle ahead. This is called echolocation (see page 28). Their hearing is so good they can hear beetles and earthworms moving in the soil.

CHIMPANZEE VS. BUSHBABY: WEAPONS

Chimpanzees are one of our closest relatives in the animal world. These intelligent animals live in social groups – sometimes more than 100 strong – in forests and savannas in Africa. Chimps eat mostly fruit and leaves, but will also hunt other animals, including small monkeys.

CLEVER KILLERS

Some female chimps have also learned that small, nocturnal primates called bushbabies, or galagos, sleep in tree-holes during the day. A hungry chimp will select a strong stick, usually about 25 inches (63.5 cm) long, and sharpen one end with its teeth to make a deadly spear. Then it will thrust it into a hole where it thinks a bushbaby is sleeping. Often, there won't be an animal inside or sometimes, the bushbaby will jump out of the hole to safety. But if the spear stabs it, the chimp has a meal.

WEAPON: AN OBJECT USED TO HARM SOMEONE OR SOMETHING

SENEGAL BUSHBABY

Bushbabies are perfectly adapted for living in total darkness. Their super-sensitive, bat-like ears can track the insects they eat. Their large eyes give them great night vision. With strong muscles in their back legs they can leap 8 feet (2.4 m) from branch to branch – or away from predators.

CHIMPANZEE STATS

Height: 4 ft (1.2 m)
Weight: 66-154 lb (30-70 kg)
Top speed: 25 mph (40 kph)

Intelligent; weapon-maker; strong

VS.

BUSHBABY STATS

Length: 5 in (13 cm)
Weight: 3.5-10 oz (100-283 g)
Top speed: unknown

Excellent night vision and hearing; fast and agile; can make long leaps

NIGHT VISION: THE ABILITY TO SEE WELL IN THE DARK

TOOLMAKERS

Chimps are incredible toolmakers. To catch termites, they use a "toolkit." First, a chimp knocks holes in the wall of the termites' nest with a large stick. Then it swaps this for a long, thin stick or blade of grass, which it pokes into the hole. When termites gather on it, the chimp whisks it out and licks them off for a snack.

HUMPBACK WHALE vs. HERRING: CONFUSION

Humpback whales live in all the world's oceans. To eat, a humpback simply opens its huge mouth as it swims. Its mouth fills with water along with any animals that may be swimming in it. Then the whale shuts it tight and pushes the water through a sieve-like structure, called a baleen plate. The animals inside – krill, fish, and small squid – are swallowed whole. These whales can go a long time without feeding, but when they do come across a shoal (group) of fish they try to eat as many as they can.

BUBBLE-NETTING

Some humpbacks have learned a clever way of getting more to eat. When they find a large shoal of fish, they dive beneath it and blow thousands of bubbles from their blowholes as they swim around and around in a circle. As the bubbles rise to the surface, they form a circular "net" that the fish are scared to swim through. The fish find themselves trapped and panic, swimming toward the surface. The whales swim up behind them with their mouths open, and swallow thousands at a time. This is called bubble-netting.

BALEEN: BRISTLE-LIKE PLATES INSIDE THE MOUTHS OF SOME WHALES

CONFUSED: BEING UNSURE OF WHAT IS HAPPENING

SHOALING BEHAVIOR

HERRING

Herring are fish that live in cool surface waters. They live in tightly packed groups, or shoals, that may contain thousands of fish. The shoals usually seem to move as one, with every individual turning at the same time to avoid predators. But they can become confused when surrounded.

HUMPBACK WHALE STATS

Length: 46-52 ft (14-16 m)
Weight: 33 tons (33 mt)
Top speed: 15 mph (24 kph)

Communicate by sound; can create bubbles with blowhole; great intelligence; team-players

VS.

HERRING STATS

Length: 10 in (25 cm)
Weight: 1 lb (0.5 kg)
Top speed: 1 mph (1.6 kph)

Excellent senses; shoaling behavior deters some predators; safety in numbers

BALEEN

A humpback whale's baleen plate hangs from its upper jaw. The flexible comb-like structure is made from keratin – the same stuff that fingernails and hair are made from. Once trapped by the baleen, a herring has no chance of escape.

BAT VS. MOTH: ECHOLOCATION

Most of the world's bats hunt flying insects at night. In the pitch darkness, being able to see is not much use to them, but that's not a problem – they use echolocation instead. Echolocation involves making a lot of noise and listening for the echoes. If you've ever shouted in a tunnel or cave you will know how this works.

BAT RADAR

As it hunts, a bat makes loud squeaks, called ultrasound. This is too high-pitched for human ears to pick up, but the bat can hear the echoes bouncing off trees, buildings – and flying prey. Incredibly, in this way the bat's brain builds up a picture of its surroundings, a bit like radar on a plane. Once it detects a prey animal, such as a moth, the bat homes in on it and snaps it up.

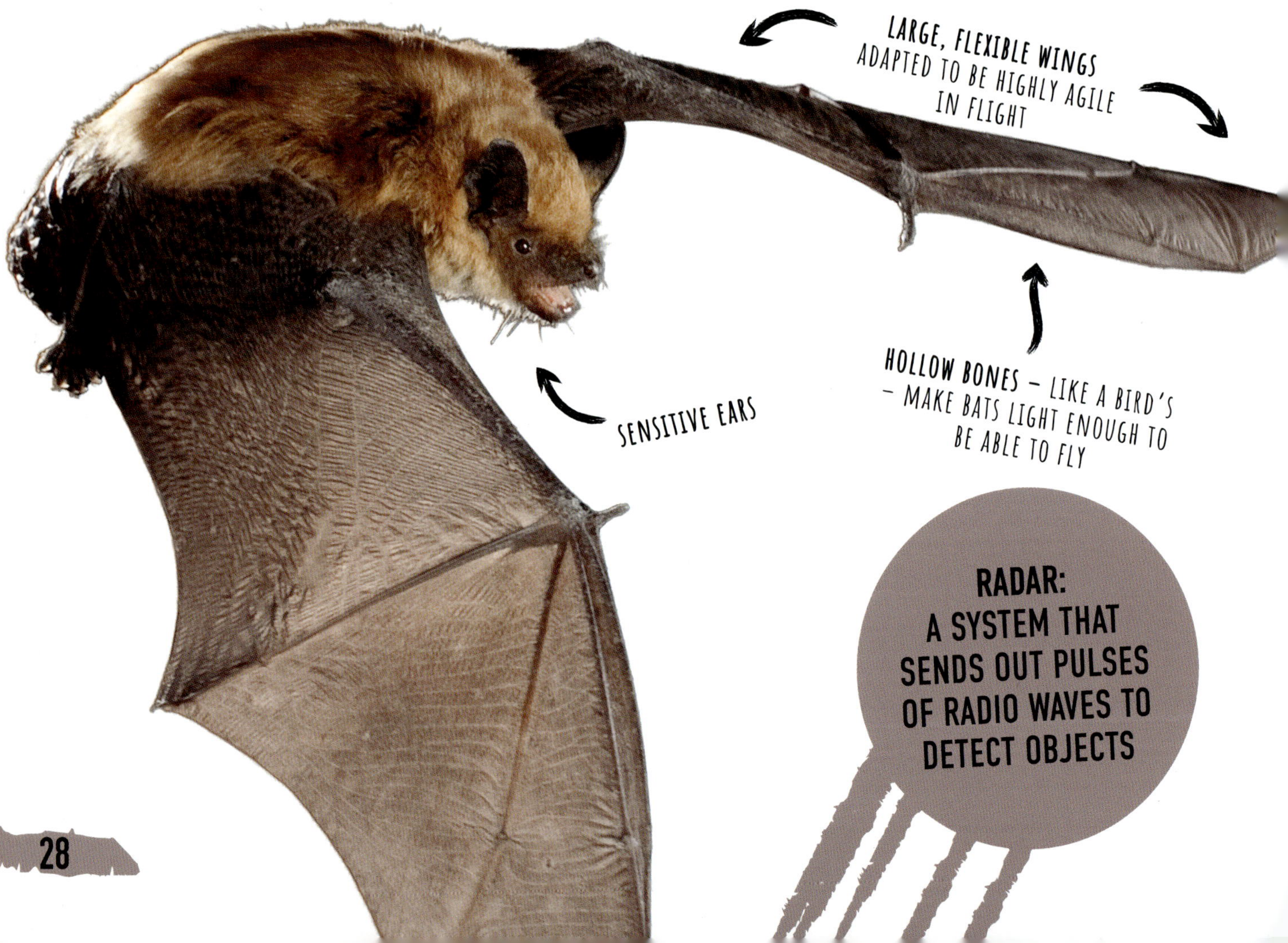

RADAR:
A SYSTEM THAT SENDS OUT PULSES OF RADIO WAVES TO DETECT OBJECTS

MOTH DEFENSES

One bat may eat thousands of moths and other invertebrates in a single night. Apart from zigzagging as they fly, most insects don't have any defense against this, but one kind of moth – the Grote's bertholdia – emits its own ultrasound clicks to confuse the bats' echolocation. It means the moth isn't actually where its echolocation says it is! This is the animal equivalent of "jamming" a radar system.

(BIG BROWN) BAT STATS

Wingspan: 12-15 in (30-38 cm)
Weight: 0.5 oz (14 g)
Top speed: 40 mph (65 kph)

Able to hunt in darkness with echolocation; very fast flight

VS.

GROTE'S BERTHOLDIA MOTH STATS

Wingspan: 0.7 in (16 mm)
Weight: less than 0.03 oz (1 g)
Top speed: unknown

Ability to use "jamming" ultrasound

PIPISTRELLE BATS ARE MUCH SMALLER THAN BIG BROWN BATS, BUT ARE JUST AS EFFICIENT AT HUNTING MOTH PREY.

GLOSSARY

alpha the dominant or lead animal in a pack or group

aquatic describes a plant or animal that grows or lives in water

binocular vision eyesight where each of the two forward-facing eyes produces an image. These images overlap to give the animal an excellent ability to judge distance and depth

camouflage fur or skin markings that help an animal to hide in its habitat

canine the long pointed teeth on either side of the front teeth in some mammals, such as big cats and dogs

capybara the world's largest rodent; it looks like a large guinea pig

carnivore an animal that eats only meat

emerge to come out of something

formidable impressive through being especially large, powerful, or scary

habitat the natural home of a plant or animal

herbivore an animal that eats only plants

hide the thick, tough skin of an animal, such as the scaly skin of a crocodile or the tough, leathery skin of a buffalo

invertebrate an animal without a backbone; spiders, insects, snails, and octopuses are all invertebrates

krill a small shrimp-like animal that is food for some marine animals, such as whales

lair a place where a wild animal lives or hides

mammal a warm-blooded animal with a backbone and that has hair or fur at some stage in its life and is fed on its mother's milk when young

marine relating to the ocean; animals that live in the ocean

predator an animal that hunts and kills other animals for food

prey/prey on an animal that is hunted for food (noun); to hunt and kill for food (verb)

regurgitate to bring up food that has already been swallowed. Some adult animals regurgitate partly-digested food for their young because it is easier for them to carry large amounts of food to them in this way and the food is softer and so easier to eat

reptile an animal with scaly skin, whose body temperature is the same as the environment around it. Reptiles may bask in the sun to warm up or seek shade to cool down

solitary describes an animal that lives alone

submerge to cover with water

suffocate to kill by cutting off its prey's air supply so it can't breathe

thrive to live or develop well

toxic describes something that is poisonous

FURTHER INFORMATION

BOOKS

Animals in Disguise by Michael Bright (Wayland, 2020)
On the Hunt with Wolves by Sandra Markle (Lerner Publications, 2023)
Visual Explorers: Predators by Toby Reynolds and Paul Calver (Franklin Watts, 2015)
Wildlife Worlds (series) by Tim Harris (Franklin Watts, 2020)
The World's Greatest Predators by Mignonne Gunasekara (Jump!, Inc., 2024)

WEBSITES

Check out the BBC bitesize website for lots of information relevant to this book and information on food chains.
www.bbc.co.uk/bitesize/topics/zx882hv/articles/z3c2xnb

National Geographic gives good introductions to the lifestyles of a range of mammals. These are some of the best pages.

Cheetahs: www.kids.nationalgeographic.com/animals/mammals/cheetah/
Chimpanzees: www.kids.nationalgeographic.com/animals/mammals/chimpanzee/
Lions: www.kids.nationalgeographic.com/animals/mammals/lion/
Orcas: www.kids.nationalgeographic.com/animals/mammals/orca/
Polar Bear: www.nationalgeographic.com/animals/mammals/p/polar-bear/
Thomson's Gazelle: www.nationalgeographic.com/animals/mammals/t/thomsons-gazelle/
Tigers: www.kids.nationalgeographic.com/animals/mammals/tiger/
Wolves: www.kids.nationalgeographic.com/animals/mammals/gray-wolf/
Zebras: www.kids.nationalgeographic.com/animals/mammals/zebra/

This is a YouTube video of jaguar attacking a caiman.
www.youtube.com/watch?v=5NrfnUfzsic

INDEX